Puppy & Kitten Math

SUBTRACTING PUPPIES and KITTENS

Patricia J. Murphy

Enslow Elementary

Contents

Words to Know

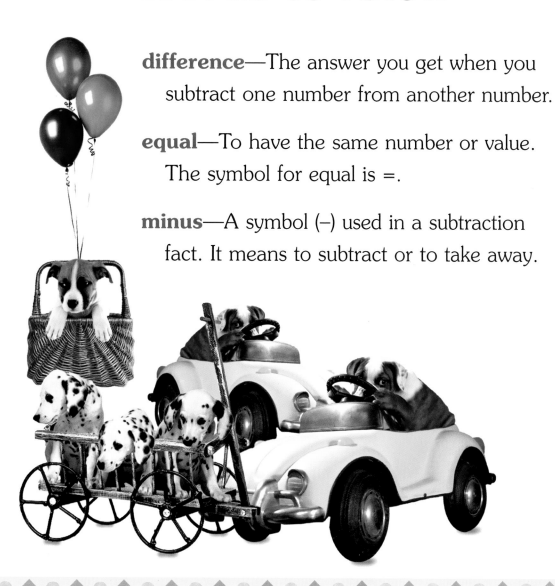

difference—The answer you get when you subtract one number from another number.

equal—To have the same number or value. The symbol for equal is =.

minus—A symbol (–) used in a subtraction fact. It means to subtract or to take away.

Taking Away

Subtracting is taking one number away from another number.
You subtract numbers to find the **difference**.

5

5 is the number you
are starting with.

2

2 is the number you
are taking away.

3

3 is the answer,
or **difference.**

You can write subtraction facts two ways:

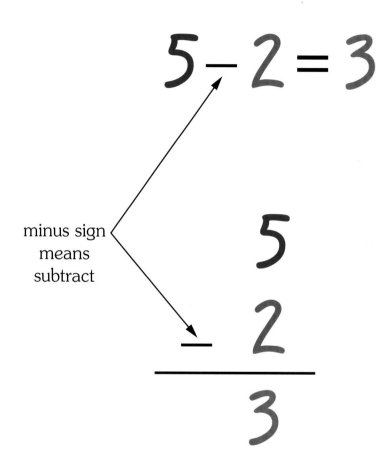

$$5 - 2 = 3$$

minus sign
means
subtract

$$\begin{array}{r} 5 \\ -\ 2 \\ \hline 3 \end{array}$$

You say "Five minus two equals three," or
"Five take away two equals three."

Subtracting 0

4 – 0

Four puppies chew a lot.   Zero puppies do not.

4   —   0

Use the
number line
to help you
subtract. Start
at 4. Go back
0 spaces. You
are still on 4.

0   1   2   3   4

How many chew a lot?

=

4

$$0 - 0 = 0$$

$$1 - 0 = 1$$

$$2 - 0 = 2$$

$$3 - 0 = 3$$

$$\mathbf{4 - 0 = 4}$$

$$5 - 0 = 5$$

$$6 - 0 = 6$$

$$7 - 0 = 7$$

$$8 - 0 = 8$$

$$9 - 0 = 9$$

$$10 - 0 = 10$$

5   6   7   8   9   10

Subtracting 1

3 – 1

Three puppies stay.   One puppy runs away.

3   1

Use the number line to help you subtract. Start at 3. Go back 1. The difference is 2.

0   1   2   3   4

How many puppies remain?

$1 - 1 = 0$

$2 - 1 = 1$

3 – 1 = 2

$4 - 1 = 3$

$5 - 1 = 4$

$6 - 1 = 5$

$7 - 1 = 6$

$8 - 1 = 7$

$9 - 1 = 8$

$10 - 1 = 9$

=

2

Subtracting 1 from any number will always make that number one less.
$5 - 1 = 4$
4 is 1 less than 5

9

5   6   7   8   9   10

Subtracting 2

6 – 2

Six puppies go to a party.

Two puppies don't dress.

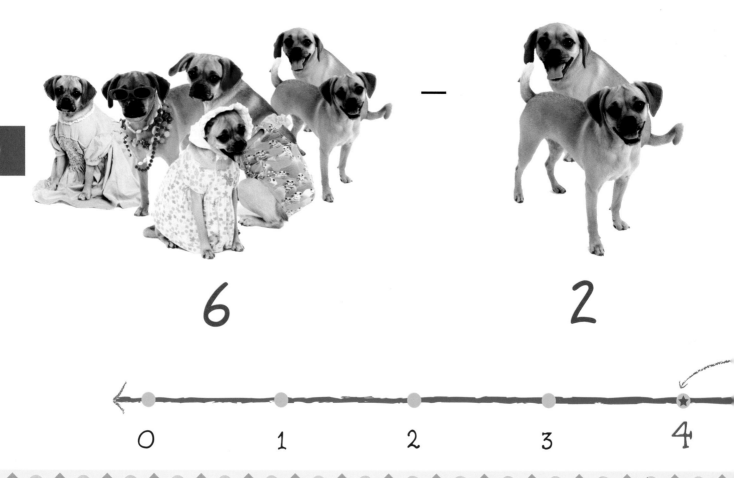

6

—

2

0   1   2   3   4

How many are left?

=

4

$$2 - 2 = 0$$
$$3 - 2 = 1$$
$$4 - 2 = 2$$
$$5 - 2 = 3$$
$$\mathbf{6 - 2 = 4}$$
$$7 - 2 = 5$$
$$8 - 2 = 6$$
$$9 - 2 = 7$$
$$10 - 2 = 8$$

5   6   7   8   9   10

Subtracting 3

5 – 3

Five kittens are in bed. Three are awake.

5 — 3

0   1   2   3   4

Counting back is one way to find answers to subtraction facts. Try counting back with 5 − 3. Start with 5, the bigger number. Then count back three numbers:

$$\overset{1}{\overset{\frown}{\quad}}\overset{2}{\overset{\frown}{\quad}}\overset{3}{\overset{\frown}{\quad}}$$
5 . . . 4 . . . 3 . . . 2
The answer is 2.

$$3 - 3 = 0$$
$$4 - 3 = 1$$
$$\mathbf{5 - 3 = 2}$$
$$6 - 3 = 3$$
$$7 - 3 = 4$$
$$8 - 3 = 5$$
$$9 - 3 = 6$$
$$10 - 3 = 7$$

How many are asleep?

=

2

5   6   7   8   9   10

13

Subtracting 4

8 – 4

Eight puppies sit in one spot.

Four have long hair.

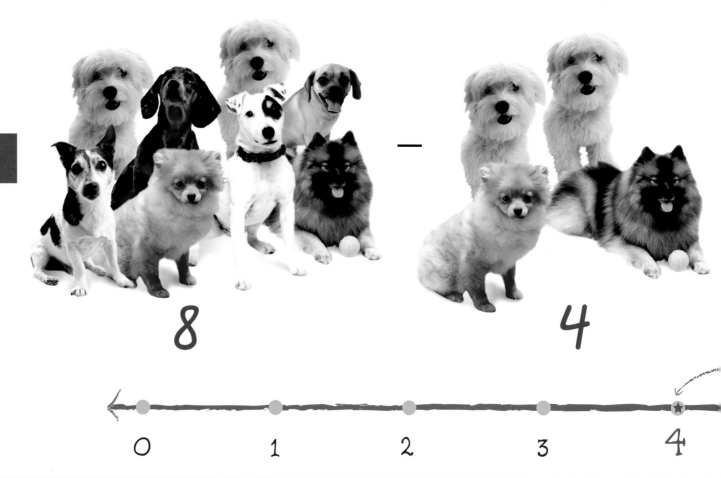

8 — 4

0   1   2   3   4

8 – 4 is a **doubles fact**. Learn these doubles and you will know 10 new subtraction facts. ⫸

2 – 1 = 1	12 – 6 = 6
4 – 2 = 2	14 – 7 = 7
6 – 3 = 3	16 – 8 = 8
8 – 4 = 4	18 – 9 = 9
10 – 5 = 5	20 – 10 = 10

4 – 4 = 0

5 – 4 = 1

6 – 4 = 2

7 – 4 = 3

8 – 4 = 4

9 – 4 = 5

10 – 4 = 6

How many do not?

=

4

5   6   7   8   9   10

Subtracting 5

7 – 5

Seven kittens start to race.

Five take a rest.

7

5

0   1   2   3   4

How many finish the race?

$$5 - 5 = 0$$
$$6 - 5 = 1$$
$$\mathbf{7 - 5 = 2}$$
$$8 - 5 = 3$$
$$9 - 5 = 4$$
$$10 - 5 = 5$$

Use addition facts that you know to find answers to subtraction facts. Here is how you do it: $7 - 5 = ?$

If you know that $5 + 2 = 7$, then you know that $7 - 5 = 2$.

=

2

5   6   7   8   9   10

Subtracting 6

10 – 6

There are ten kittens.

Six are black.

10

6

0   1   2   3   4

How many are white?

4

$$6 - 6 = 0$$
$$7 - 6 = 1$$
$$8 - 6 = 2$$
$$9 - 6 = 3$$
$$\mathbf{10 - 6 = 4}$$

Learn all your subtraction facts up to 10.

10 – 0 = 10	10 – 6 = 4
10 – 1 = 9	10 – 7 = 3
10 – 2 = 8	10 – 8 = 2
10 – 3 = 7	10 – 9 = 1
10 – 4 = 6	10 – 10 = 0
10 – 5 = 5	

5   6   7   8   9   10

Subtracting 7

9 – 7

Nine puppies are hungry.

Seven wait.

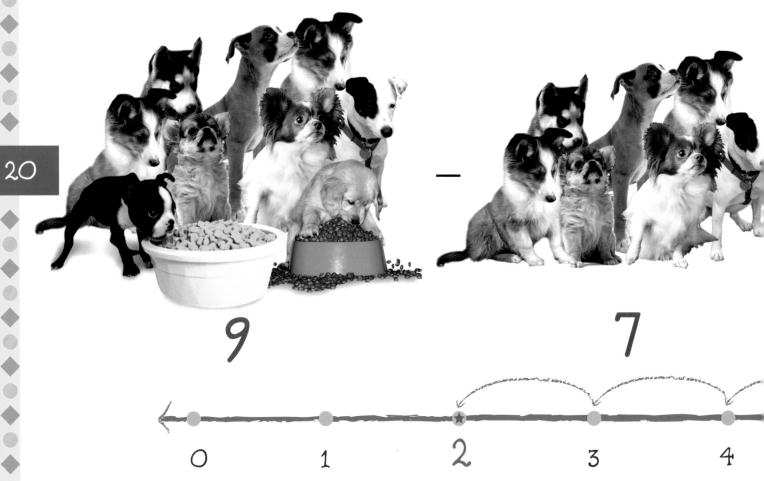

9

—

7

0   1   2   3   4

How many eat?

$$7 - 7 = 0$$
$$8 - 7 = 1$$
$$\mathbf{9 - 7 = 2}$$
$$10 - 7 = 3$$

=

When you know one
subtraction fact, you really know
four math facts!
These facts are called a fact family:

$$9 - 7 = 2 \qquad 9 - 2 = 7$$
$$7 + 2 = 9 \qquad 2 + 7 = 9$$

2

5   6   7   8   9   10

Subtracting 8

10 – 8

Ten puppies live on a farm.

Eight puppies take a ride.

10

8

0   1   2   3   4

How many stay behind?

$$8 - 8 = 0$$
$$9 - 8 = 1$$
$$\mathbf{10 - 8 = 2}$$

=

2

5   6   7   8   9   10

Subtracting 9
10 – 9

There are ten kittens in all.

Nine kittens sit.

10 — 9

0   1   2   3   4

How many
stand tall?

$$9 - 9 = 0$$
$$\mathbf{10 - 9 = 1}$$

=

1

You can also *count on* to find answers
to subtraction facts.

$$10 - 9$$

Start with 9, the smaller number. Then count up to 10.
9 . . . 10

The answer is 1 because you had to count
up one number to get from 9 to 10.

5   *6*   *7*   *8*   *9*   *10*

Subtracting 10

10 – 10

Ten puppies have a play date.

10

—

0   1   2   3   4

Ten are on time.

$$10 - 10 = 0$$

How many are late?

$$=$$

10

0

5   6   7   8   9   10

Looking Back

Take another look at the subtraction facts in this book.

−0
1 − 0 = 1	4 − 0 = 4	7 − 0 = 7	9 − 0 = 9
2 − 0 = 2	5 − 0 = 5	8 − 0 = 8	10 − 0 = 10
3 − 0 = 3	6 − 0 = 6		

−1
1 − 1 = 0	4 − 1 = 3	7 − 1 = 6	9 − 1 = 8
2 − 1 = 1	5 − 1 = 4	8 − 1 = 7	10 − 1 = 9
3 − 1 = 2	6 − 1 = 5		

−2
2 − 2 = 0	5 − 2 = 3	8 − 2 = 6
3 − 2 = 1	6 − 2 = 4	9 − 2 = 7
4 − 2 = 2	7 − 2 = 5	10 − 2 = 8

−3
3 − 3 = 0	6 − 3 = 3	9 − 3 = 6
4 − 3 = 1	7 − 3 = 4	10 − 3 = 7
5 − 3 = 2	8 − 3 = 5	

−4
4 − 4 = 0	7 − 4 = 3	9 − 4 = 5
5 − 4 = 1	8 − 4 = 4	10 − 4 = 6
6 − 4 = 2		

−5

5 − 5 = 0   8 − 5 = 3
6 − 5 = 1   9 − 5 = 4
7 − 5 = 2   10 − 5 = 5

−6

6 − 6 = 0   9 − 6 = 3
7 − 6 = 1   10 − 6 = 4
8 − 6 = 2

−7

7 − 7 = 0   9 − 7 = 2
8 − 7 = 1   10 − 7 = 3

−8

8 − 8 = 0
9 − 8 = 1
10 − 8 = 2

−9

9 − 9 = 0
10 − 9 = 1

−10

10 − 10 = 0

Ways to Keep Subtracting

Write Your Own Subtraction Book

Use paper, pencils, and crayons to write your own subtraction book. On each page, write a different subtraction fact. Draw a picture to go with each fact. Put the pages together. Share your book with friends.

Subtraction Attraction!

Wherever you find big and little numbers, subtract them! Subtract numbers in speed limits, numbers in stores, and numbers of your phone number. Make up your own subtraction problems and share them with others.

SPEED LIMIT 40

Take Away, Okay?

Use a pair of dice or playing cards to play this game. Take turns rolling the dice or flipping over the dominoes or cards with a friend. Write down the two numbers you roll or uncover and make subtraction facts with them. Take turns answering the subtraction facts.

Learn More

Books

Bryant, Megan E. *Apples Away!* New York: Grosset & Dunlap, 2003.

Franco, Betsy. *Subtraction Fun.* Mankato, Minn.: Yellow Umbrella Books, 2002.

Leedy, Loreen. *Subtraction Action.* New York: Holiday House, 2000.

Murphy, Stuart J. *Monster Musical Chairs.* New York: HarperCollins Publishers, 2000.

———. *Shark Swimathon*. New York: HarperCollins, 2001.

O'Donnell, Kerri. *Explorers in North America: Solving Addition and Subtraction Problems Using Timelines*. New York: PowerKids Press, 2004.

Pallotta, Jerry. *The Hershey's Kisses Subtraction Book*. New York: Scholastic, 2002.

Web Sites

AAA Math: Subtraction.
<http://www.321know.com/sub.htm>

Fun Brain Numbers.
<http://www.funbrain.com/numbers.html>

A Plus Math.
<http://www.aplusmath.com>

Index

Series Math Consultant
Eileen Fernández, Ph.D.
Associate Professor, Mathematics Education
Montclair State University
Montclair, NJ

Series Literacy Consultant
Allan A. De Fina, Ph.D.
Past President of the New Jersey Reading Association
Professor, Department of Literacy Education
New Jersey City University
Jersey City, NJ

In memory of Bailey, Ginger, Sam, and Tuffy

Acknowledgments: The author thanks Arlington Heights School District #25, in Arlington Heights, IL, and Lake Forest School District #67, in Lake Forest, IL, for their assistance in the research of this book.

Enslow Elementary, an imprint of Enslow Publishers, Inc.

Enslow Elementary® is a registered trademark of Enslow Publishers, Inc.

Library of Congress Cataloging-in-Publication Data

Murphy, Patricia J., 1963–
   Subtracting puppies and kittens / by Patricia J. Murphy.
      p. cm. — (Puppy and kitten math)
   Includes bibliographical references and index.
   ISBN-13: 978-0-7660-2725-1
   ISBN-10: 0-7660-2725-2
   1. Subtraction—Juvenile literature. 2. Arithmetic—Juvenile literature. I. Title.
   QA115.M8587 2006
   513.2'12—dc22   2006004873

Printed in the United States of America

10 9 8 7 6 5 4 3 2 1

To Our Readers: We have done our best to make sure all Internet Addresses in this book were active and appropriate when we went to press. However, the author and the publisher have no control over and assume no liability for the material available on those Internet sites or on other Web sites they may link to. Any comments or suggestions can be sent by e-mail to comments@enslow.com or to the address on the back cover.

Photo credits: Hemera Technologies, pp. 3 in wagon, basket, 12–13 bed, 27 clock, 31; Jane Burton/Photo Researchers, Inc., pp. 1 left, 24, 25; ©Jupiterimages Corporation, pp. 20 bottom left, 21; ©iStockphoto.com, pp. 4 puppies, 5 #3, 26–27 far left; ©iStockphoto.com, pp. 18 white, 19 (Anne Gro Bergersen), 26–27 with ball (Antti Karppinen), 14 #8: top furry puppies, #4: top (Byron Carlson), 20 shetland (Dan Brandenburg), 20 black and white (Elena Slastnova), 14 #8: third on bottom, 15 bottom right (Fielding Piepereit), 26–27 top left (Jackson Gee), 14 bottom left, 15 bottom left (Jurgen van de Pol), 8 third from right (Justin Horrocks), 20 jack russell (Lynn Watson), 10 sunglasses, 11 sunglasses, 28 (Rick Orrell), 26–27 far right (Scott Waite), 6 right, 7 right (Steve Strawn), 20 boxer (Tad Denson), 6 left, 7 left (Verity Johnson), 26–27 second from right (Wee Gan Peng); Shutterstock, pp. 1, 3 puppy in car, puppy in basket, 4 kittens, 5 #2, 8 two at far left, 9, 10 all but sunglasses, 11 all but sunglasses, 12–13 kittens, 14 #8: column 2 & 4, #4: top, 15 top, 16, 17, 18 black, 20 chihuahuas, 26–27 bottom left, top right, top center; © Tom Rosenthal/Superstock, pp. 22–23; ©Twuelfing/Dreamstime.com, p. 8 #1; © Warren Photographics, p. 29.

Cover photo: © Warren Photographics

Enslow Elementary
an imprint of
Enslow Publishers, Inc.
40 Industrial Road
Box 398
Berkeley Heights, NJ 07922
USA

http://www.enslow.com